IMAGES
of England

BEIGHTON

St Mary's church, Beighton. This is a view from the north side with the vicarage on the right and the home of Lucretia Smith (queen of the gypsies) in the centre.

IMAGES
of England

BEIGHTON

Compiled by
Julia E. Siddons and Leonard Widdowson

TEMPUS

First published 1998
Copyright © Julia E. Siddons and Leonard Widdowson, 1998

Tempus Publishing Limited
The Mill, Brimscombe Port,
Stroud, Gloucestershire, GL5 2QG

ISBN 0 7524 1162 4

Typesetting and origination by
Tempus Publishing Limited
Printed in Great Britain by
Midway Clark Printing, Wiltshire

Flooding in Beighton.

Contents

No.1117. High Street. Beighton.

High Street.

Acknowledgements

Many thanks to Rodger Siddons for typing and re-typing all our work. Thank you to Stan Fox and Ben Clayton for their pictures and a special thanks to Horace York for letting us have Olive's pictures, for without them this book would not have been published.

Introduction

I wonder if you would like to come with me on a journey around Beighton remembering some of the sites that have disappeared. Did you know we had a castle and a queen in our midst? The castle was in the fields to the right, going up to Swallownest near where Tommy Wards is now, and the queen was the queen of the gypsies, who is buried in the churchyard. She lived in a cottage on Tye Lane with her daughter Matilda Boswell. It is said that the queen was a truly good person who helped the sick and gave money to the poor. On her death hundreds of gypsies came to Beighton to pay their respects to a lady who was well loved.

At one time we had a Lord of the Manor, to whom we paid rents, and the village was surrounded by fields. Then Beighton was a part of Derbyshire, later we had our own parish council to look after all our needs, now we are part of Sheffield. On the road going up to Swallownest there used to be a gasworks, a flour mill and a paper mill. There was a station too and steam trains would pass through the village. There was a coal pit and coke ovens where quite a few of our men worked and a brickyard in the village producing Beighton bricks, but all this has gone. We had our own coat of arms.

Quite a few people know what we mean when we refer to 'Beighton by the Sea'; this was when the River Rother flooded. We had water coming right up to Woodhouse Lane and the High Street, which meant the men had to use rather different modes of transport to get to their places of work.

Most streets had a corner shop where all the local gossip could be exchanged. There was a cinema where some of the latest films were shown and we had to queue up on a Saturday night for the two houses because they were so popular. When the cinema closed, it was converted into a bingo hall, Elsie Tanner of *Coronation Street* came to open it. We can still recognise most of the pubs today as they have changed very little and only two others have been opened in more recent times.

Many people used the train for going to Sheffield as it was quicker than the bus. No doubt many people reading this will remember travelling by train to Cleethorpes. Those were the days!

Beighton didn't escape the war. Bombs and landmines were dropped around the village but fortunately they caused no serious damage. In February 1942 a troop train carrying nearly 400 troops crashed just outside Beighton Station, two local doctors, Dr de Dombel and Dr Lipp worked most of the night to help the injured.

Beighton is an ancient Anglo-Saxon settlement. It is mentioned twice in the Domesday survey of 1086, ordered by King William the Conqueror so that he knew exactly how much land each man had and what tax payments were due to him. The first documentary notice of Beighton however occurs early in Saxon times, in the will of one Wilfric Spott in 1002. He appears to have been an officer attached to the court of King Ethelred the second. At that time Beighton was known as Bectune, Bectun or Becton, but there was no mention of a church. The discovery of a Norman arch, during massive restoration work on the church in the last century, confirmed its Norman origins dating back to about 1150. The church first appears on record as 'St Radegund of Bectun' in the thirteenth century. Radegund was the daughter of a Thuringian prince (an area of the new united Germany) and lived from 518 to 587 AD. The exact date when the church was dedicated to St Mary is not known, however it was referred to as St Radegund in 1553 and St Mary's in 1583.

What changes have occurred since the days of the Domesday survey, a time when the population of the whole of Derbyshire was only 3,041. Since then coal mines have been sunk and closed. Many will remember the sound of clogs and the black faces of the miners coming home after a shift, before the pit head baths were built. Traction engines and threshing machines no longer come to the farms, those farms have gone and the land they occupied has been used for building. The annual feast was held on the Miners Welfare Grounds every second week in August, a traditional holiday time for the men employed at the pit and coke ovens. Until the railway station closed on 1 November 1954, there were club outings to the coast by coaches and by train. Processions and Gala days and the less pleasant experiences of war time and the damage and inconvenience caused by the floods during prolonged heavy rain are now thankfully a thing of the past. We don't have fields round Beighton any more but Crystal Peaks has become quite a focal point where old Beighton folks meet and catch up with the gossip, so perhaps not everything is bad!

Many of the pictures included here are of times when life went on at a more leisurely pace, when we travelled on unlit roads into the next village at night and Beighton had its own parish council. This was a time when everybody had a Co-op number and they knew the names and pedigree of every family from one end of the road to the other.

The majority of these pictures came from Olive York, a late member of our society, who was well known in Beighton. We are always on the lookout for new pictures, so please don't forget, let us have any you can spare, we will return them after taking a print.

We hope that this book gives as much pleasure to you as it has to us in compiling it.

J.E. Siddons and L. Widdowson
1998

An Old Beighton Poem

Beighton is a pretty place
and righteous it should be.
For it can boast a rare old church
and chapels one, two, three.
But it is not a noted spot
so spread its fame around
a Queen lies buried here within
the sacred burial ground.

One
High Street

High Street, c. 1885. The empty carts outside the blacksmiths shop await the return of their horses. The row of buildings on the left have now been replaced with a more uniform row of shops. The George and Dragon, visible in the distance, was demolished several years ago. The new public house is built further back from the road, the vacated land now forming part of the car park.

This was known as Tomlinson's shop, situated on the corner of Rotherham Road and High Street. It was always busy with local shoppers and passing coal miners as well as people using the nearby railway station.

Pleasant's shop at the bottom of Queens Road in 1953. It had previously been Abbott's shop. Today it is a hairdressing salon.

To the left of Pleasant's shop stood this stone row of cottages, always referred to as Miles Row. Most, if not all, of the occupants had left by this time, prior to the demolition of the buildings. The George and Dragon and its car park now occupy much of this land.

By 1907 a new row of shops had been erected. The George and Dragon public house, seen behind the cart, was kept by Harry Hutton.

Looking along High Street from the opposite end of the row of shops, we can see the entrance to the large house known as The Grange.

Mattson's was a well known shoe shop. The premises are now occupied by Ossie Bennett's car spares shop which is equally well known.

This is the bottom of Grange Road where the old wash-house and the coach house, which belonged to The Grange, stand.

A 1950s view, during the widening of Grange Road.

This large building is The Grange. Today modern semi-detached houses occupy the land.

This lane, which ran from High Street alongside the Ochre Dyke, formed the ancient road through Beighton on to Sothal and up to Hackenthorpe.

The bridge on Ivy Lane crosses the Ochre Dyke and leads up to Tye Lane. Here stood the ancient pack horse bridge which is mentioned in a document in the British Museum dated 1328.

These are the Little Hill steps leading up to Tye Lane and the parish church from the bridge below.

The forty one steps to the church yard.

This horse trough stands at the end of Ivy Lane.

Frank Money crosses the
Ochre Dyke on his way to
deliver mail to Revilles
cottages.

Beighton cinema was a big attraction, it was built in 1913 by Tom Staveley and E. Whitley. There were always queues to get in for every performance. Mrs Bland, Mrs Fanthorpe and Mrs Norris were among those waiting.

Central Cinema in 1963. The crowd of people have gathered to await the arrival of Pat Phoenix (Elsie Tanner of *Coronation Street* fame). The cinema was about to be reopened as a bingo hall.

This old farmhouse on Tye Lane once belonged to Earl Manvers, Lord of the Manor of Beighton and he collected his village rents twice a year from here. In the late 1800s the house had an adjoining piece built on, to be used as a joiners shop. At one time it had been a tailors shop before becoming a farm, belonging to Rowbottoms.

These shops are still recognisable today as the post office and Lowes paper shop. In the 1950s they accommodated Fanthorpe's bakers and the Woodhouse Co-op.

Looking up the High Street there were market stalls in the Royal Oaks car park, where we are told that 'a bear came and performed and slept, with its owner, in out-houses belonging to the pub'. Colliers Row can be seen higher up the hill on the right, where the buttress is.

Another of our old shops, c. 1890. At that time this was the only shop in the village and was kept by Joseph Lowe. It was both post office and general store, later it became Money's then Peckhams and is now a private house.

Dr Fordyce lived at The Beeches. In later years part of the building was used as the village library.

This is a view looking up the High Street from The Beeches, *c.* 1930.

This old shop on High Street was a saddlers in 1871, a hat shop in 1895, a watch makers in the 1920s, a china shop in the 1930s, a cobblers and shoe shop in the 1970s, a wine shop and then a video shop. After such a wide variety of occupants, it is now a private house.

Half way down the High Street this was known as saddler Bank's shop, but I knew it as Williams coal merchants.

The yard of The Beeches, home of Dr Fordyce, *c.* 1910. We no longer see doctors going to visit patients around the village in a pony and trap. Arthur and Charlie Fenton are pictured here.

This was Grange Farm, just beyond The Beeches. It now has a name plate calling it The Long House.

These are among the oldest houses in Beighton, some of the windows have been replaced, but little else thank goodness. The families of Keeton, Rhodes and Jarvis lived here. The houses stand on the right going up High Street.

A quiet scene looking down High Street with the Cumberland Head public house on the left. Opposite is The Beeches, now demolished, but remembered in the naming of Beeches Grove, a new road off the High Street.

24

This view of High Street shows both sides of the street.

Within living memory this has always been a butchers shop. It has now sadly closed and has been converted along with adjacent property, into private houses in recent years.

Another old cottage in the High Street, behind the building society. It was built in 1734 and was a farm. A well was found in the garden during renovation work.

Wilkinson's shop. Many children would call in before school asking for 1d worth of coconut or cocoa and sugar.

Two more of our old houses at the top of High Street, built before the eighteenth century. They were Manor Farm cottages where farm labourers lived.

The church hall was built in 1892. Three cottages once stood on this site. So even in those days buildings were pulled down and the sites redeveloped! Note the bell tower, it was lost only last year when the hall was re-roofed.

Opposite the church hall is the Manor Farm which once belonged to Simon Pierpoint, Lord of the Manor.

The second vicarage was built in the early 1900s. The first vicarage being situated in the church yard. In its place today stands a new nursing home.

Two
Sothall and West Street

This pair of cottages at the beginning of Eckington Road was built for the families of the workmen employed at the nearby quarry.

This house stands at the junction of West Street and Eckington Road and was the gate house to the quarry.

Looking along Eckington Road from its junction with West Street, c. 1900.

E.L.S. 212-9. Beighton.

Another early view of Eckington Road, known locally as 'The Cutting'. The vicarage is in the background. Note how narrow the road was when it was first cut through the solid rock.

Mr Swift is sitting on the front wheel of the engine that helped to cut Eckington Road through. Prior to this, traffic from the High Street had to travel via West Street and Orchard Lane to join the road to Halfway and Eckington.

West Street, look how many shops we had then. This was at a time when there were no supermarkets. In the 1870s there were only four houses between the Free Church and Orchard Lane. Branch No. 2 of the Woodhouse Co-operative Society is on the right.

A much more crowded view of West Street during the Gala celebrations in 1953. Mr Billam, in Scouts uniform, proudly leads the parade. The Sothall Club on the right has now extended into the open space.

The Ochre Dyke winds its way through the fields behind West Street. It takes its name from the ochre colour of the water, which was acquired as a result of the mine workings in the area. On the skyline the church and church hall can be seen, just to the left of the now demolished vicarage.

This is the bottom of Sothall Green showing Orchard Lane on the left, with Black's bakery and Howson's shop at the bottom of Allen Road. The long row of houses, with Stallard's shop at the end has since been demolished.

Mr and Mrs Keeton's newsagents shop.

Fred Cross' shop was burnt down in 1928. Lots of children watched the fire, but Mr Felstead arrived with his cane to send them home.

The children's playground at Sothall, in 1942. The land is now occupied by modern houses. The church tower can be discerned through the foliage of the tree in the centre of the picture.

When the flat-roofed houses were built in Armstead Road they were thought to be very modern.

The house with the ladder dated from 1707 and was built by G. Jessop. Further down Sothall Green was The Laurels, where Sothall Close is now.

A further picture of Sothall Green. The houses on the right are still the same but the clothes the children are wearing differ widely from today's fashions. The building on the left has since been demolished.

36

A view of the frontage of the large house known as The Laurels. Sadly this fine building in Sothall Green has been demolished.

The Laurels, once known as the White House. There were stables and kennels for horses and hounds, which were regularly used for fox hunting. Mr and Mrs Lister lived here through the turn of the century when the house was named Beighton Villa. The Glovers lived there in the 1920s, Bully Smith and the Bennetts in the 1930s and '40s and the Summers from 1950 to 1960, when it was demolished.

This cottage on the left going up Sothall Green was once the coach house to The Laurels. Mr and Mrs Staniforth and family lived there for quite a number of years and nowadays it is often referred to as Staniforth's bungalow by local people.

Ayles Garth, in 1978. This house in Sothall Green was built from bricks left over from the paper mill on Rotherham Road, which was demolished in 1926.

Reignhead Farm on Sothall Green was a busy farm. Although it still exists much of the land has now been used for building. The nearby new school takes its name from the farm.

The cows at Reignhead Farm look out on Sothall Green.

Rose Cottage was another very old cottage on Sothall Green. The year 1707 was etched on the key stone over the door.

This detached cottage was built well back off Robin Lane in 1724. It was most probably a small farmhouse, with its own wells to supply water. It is often referred to as Tyson's house from the family who lived there for many years. The access drive is at the side of the shop on Robin Lane.

Skelton Lane looking towards Robin Lane and Reignhead Farm. This was called Well Lane in the 1800s, taking its name from the fact that there were quite a few springs, ponds and wells.

Hawthorn Lodge. The house stood on the left hand side of Skelton Lane as one looks in the same direction as the photograph above. The house has since been demolished.

Herbert Renshaw poses in the doorway of his father's well stocked butchers shop. The shop stood on the left going up Orchard Lane.

Note the old telegraph poles and gas lamp in this view of Orchard Lane.

Drakehouse Lane, in 1900. The earth surface of the road shows up the numerous cart tracks in this picture, taken at the point where the Ochre Dyke passes under the road. The water in the gutter suggests overnight rain. The line of washing seems to indicate that it was a still day.

Mr and Mrs Tomlinson built the last Drakehouse and lived there for a few years. The last occupant was Dr McMillan. After he left the house was boarded up, it was eventually pulled down in around 1988 to make way for the car park opposite Crystal Peaks.

This was the second Drakehouse, built in 1890. This was where Captain Johnson, a veterinary surgeon and John Jubb, a farmer and school governor lived. A new Drakehouse was built on the same site where Tomlinsons, a well known Beighton builder lived for some years.

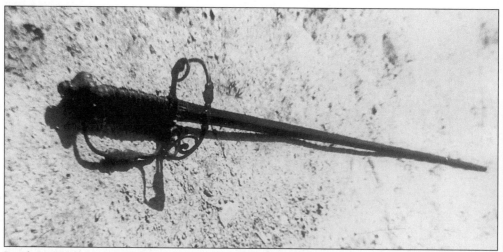

Beighton Drakehouse Sword was featured on *The Antiques Roadshow*, when the programme was broadcast from Guildford on 12 February 1989. This sword originally belonged to the Jermyn family who lived at the first Drakehouse in the late seventeenth century. It then later passed through marriage to the Huttons, a well known Ridgeway family who were for many years the owners of a scythe and sickle industry at the Phoenix Works.

Three
Robin Lane and Queens Road

Here we see evidence of work being carried out for the laying of pipes on the right hand side of Robin Lane in 1910.

A lone cyclist could safely use the centre of the road in those days. Note the large pole on the left and its position on the previous page.

Queens Road top in 1910. There were no cars about in those days, so a large group of children can safely stand and watch the photographer.

An early view lower down Queens Road shows three gas lamps upto the curb only on the left hand side of the road. With the coming of the railway in the valley and the village having its own station, Queens Road was originally known as Station Road.

This is the corner of Robin Lane and Queens Road, where a row of buildings known as Elm cottages stood.

The houses on the right hand side of Oak Road are long gone. Manvers Road can be seen in the background. Race's shop is on the corner.

The opposite side of Oak Road is pictured. These houses were demolished shortly afterwards.

Matthews off licence and general stores was possibly the most well known corner shop in the village. Unfortunately it has since closed its doors - a sign of the times!

The junction of Elm Road with Queens Road, pictured on a winter day. At that time butcher, A. Noden, occupied the shop on the left.

This was Noden's butchers shop, near the bottom of Queens Road, *c.* 1907. What about the meat! Mr and Mrs Noden and Alice are pictured in the doorways with Arthur Jones looking after the horse and trap. The sides of meat hung to either side of the window would not meet with health regulations these days.

Manvers Road contained houses built for the people working at the pit, they were known as Company Houses.

Starsmore's shop on Manvers Road is just a memory now.

Arthur Starsmore had this shop in Manvers Road selling the latest fashions in clothes, *c.* 1912.

These derelict houses were on the side of Garden Walk. The area is now occupied by the flats behind the George & Dragon.

Looking up Garden Walk where George Mirfin had his workshops. Garden Walk connected High Street with Manvers Road.

Reddish bricks were made in the brickyard on Queens Road using clay from the pond hole on Manvers Road.

A couple is pictured near the bottom of Grange Road at its junction with High Street, c. 1950. The pavilion of the Beighton Miners Welfare Sports Ground can be seen in the background as well as the open space where a fair was held every year in the second week of August.

This was Groves Farm in the 1800s, a golf house in the 1920s and then became the Miners Welfare in 1927. Drapers Dance Hall now occupies the site.

The old Linley Farm was on Woodhouse Lane. The land is now occupied by the road and houses of Rothervale Close.

Here are two of the four houses known as The Terrace. One of the other two became a gas showroom. Now we have Tulip Tree Close in their place.

H. & O. Yorks grocery shop has since closed and been converted into a private residence.

Molinairies house and ice cream shop, at the junction of Robin Lane and Woodhouse Lane.

This shows a row of ten of the twenty-four houses known as Norcroft Cottages.

A further picture showing some of the Norcroft Cottages.

Cliff Wheel Road, c. 1910. The gate on the right gave access to the path where the water-driven wheel and dams were. It was one of five sites in the Shirebrook Valley where in the last century scythes, sickles and edge tools were forged and ground.

A tunnel was found at the bottom of Cliff Wheel during construction of the new by-pass.

Looking towards Cliff Wheel from Linley Bank, you can see Seldom Seen cottages in the distance. The site of Cliff Wheel is now covered by a landfill site, the road has been straightened and raised and it crosses the link road from the Mosborough Parkway to the Aston by-pass at a large roundabout.

Four
Pubs and Advertisements

The Cumberland's Head in 1895, with a few of their customers outside. Behind here was Colliers Row. Note the lion in the right hand window, also note George Valantine Bowers' name is over the door. Other landlords have included Thomas Turton (1846-57), Alfred Hydes (1859), Wm Crooks (1861), Wm Cooper (1868-72), John Mirfin (1879-81), F. Morley (1895), G.V. Bowers (1895), Wm James John (1908-10), Mrs Rose Emily John (1914-40), Mrs Ivy Lowe (1944-48), Herbert Lowe (1951), Reg Levic (1953-63), Arthur Allcock (1963-72), Joe Siddall (1972-91) who came from the Halfway Hotel when it was demolished. Roger Sidwell is the present landlord.

The Cumberland's Head again in 1895. F. Morley's name adorns the signboard now. Looking down the High Street you can see a buttress supporting a wall which has only recently been removed. Further down you can see that at that time there were no shops at the bottom.

The Cumberland's Head in more recent times, quite a few more buildings are now visible in the background. The two bay windows give added room space to a public house which has otherwise changed little in outside appearance since the Don Brewery supplied 'Sparkling Ales'.

Before the bay windows were built on the Cumberland's Head this lion stood on the window ledge.

The first George & Dragon was built in 1780 and was called the Kingston Arms. The name changed in the 1800s and was often called 'the low drop' by locals. The landlords included Wm Watts (1827), Hannah Watts (1846), George Scholfield (1857-61), Ed Turton (1871-95), Harry Hutton (1908-09), Williamson Glover (1910-30), Mrs Mary Glover (1935-40), Leonard Ansell (1944-54), Frank Johnson (1954-59), John Weaver (1959-65), Phil Mulvaney (1965-69), Laurence Walker (1972) and in more recent times Colin Bradshaw, Paul Marshell and now Glyn Smith.

This is the second George and Dragon, but not the last – we have a third building now.

When visiting BEIGHTON
Comfort and Civility
awaits you at—

"The George & Dragon"
Proprietor: LEN ANSELL.

BRAMPTON'S FINE ALES

Wines : *Spirits*

BILLIARDS & SNOOKER

———

Opposite the Football Ground.

The Railway Inn was surrounded by water every time the River Rother overflowed its banks, which occurred during prolonged heavy rain. The Railway Inn was a Mappings house. Mappings Brewery was on Greasbough Road, Rotherham. In 1954 Mappings were taken over by Stones Brewery of Sheffield.

Railway Inn in 1953. Landlords were Thos Murfin (1846-59), Wm Boaler (1861), Mrs Ann Boaler (1868-84) Hy A.M. Boaler (1895-1909), Wm Wells (1910), John Wilson (1914-20), Hy Aaron Morris (1921-30), R. Wright (1935-40), Mrs Wright (1944-48), Mrs Mary Widdowson (1951). The last landlord was Mr Rylett who later moved into the newly built Fox Inn on Robin Lane.

The Royal Oak in 1914. No horses are left outside these days. Here we see Reubin Walters with his horse and cart and George Banks, the landlord, in the doorway. Landlords for the years from 1846 to '95 were John Crookes, Wm Crookes, Charles Crookes. Others were George Banks (1908-14), Arthur Cutts (1920), Frank Rogers (1925-27), Mrs Agnes Taylor (1928), Charles Holden (1929-30), Hy A. Morris (1935), Charles Stevenson (1940) Wm Widdison then Mrs Widdison (1944-64), Fred Ball (1956-65), Joe Ashton (1965-67), Wm Turner (1967). Chris Pearce took over after Wm Turner retired. The present landlords are Bill and Gaynor Earnshaw.

A more modern photograph of the Royal Oak. It hasn't changed much.

The Fox Inn on Robin Lane in 1953. This was shortly after it was built by C.M. Smith. The license from the demolished Railway Inn was transferred to this pub. Mr Rylett became the first landlord and others that have followed include Terence J. Cooke, John Horsfield, Eric Pass. Karen Cook is presently the landlady.

Enlarged and modernised, The Fox is seen here forty years later.

Some pottery had a Beighton coat of arms painted on it in the 1920s. The symbols represented old Beighton; the colliery, miners with pick and lamps and the church. A golf club and balls are crossed by a riding crop on the top of the pot. The crop signifies the existence of a nineteenth-century racecourse in the village. The lion was an emblem from the coat of arms of the Earl Manvers, who was the Lord of the Manor.

A matching cup and saucer, bearing the Beighton coat of arms. These were sold at Drapers village shop in the 1920s.

Five
Churches and Chapels

In the parish church can be seen this painting of c. 1840.

The small house in front of the church is where Lucretia Smith, queen of the gypsies lived. She and her daughter Matilda Boswell are buried in the churchyard.

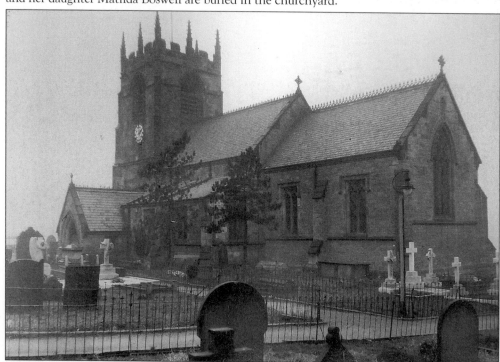

The church is Norman in origin, dating from about 1150. It was dedicated to St Radegund who was the daughter of a Thuringian prince and lived from 518 to 587. The church was later dedicated to St Mary the Virgin. The clock was mounted in the tower as a memorial to the men who died in the First World War, the lychgate being erected to the men who lost their lives in the Second World War.

E.L.S. 212-3. Interior, Beighton Church.

A view of the interior of the church with oil lighting, *c.* 1901. The east window is dedicated to the memory of Marietta Stone, who died in infancy on 26 August 1868, and her sister, Agnes Wilson (1864-81).

This shows the interior of the church in 1909, now illuminated by gas lighting.

These are some of the Boswell family who were relatives of Lucretia Smith.

In the churchyard, to the left of the path coming down from Church Lane end and just beyond the path leading to the church, is the grave of the Lucretia Smith and her daughter Matilda Boswell. The gypsy queen died in 1844.

Though still known as the forty-one steps, today there are only thirty-nine steps leading up to the church. The steps were built by the nuns and monks who brought their wares to the village. Notice the different dress of the people in the picture.

Outside the church, on the tower, is this masons mark. Try walking round and see if you can find it.

The church on West Street was built in 1870-71 to seat about 200 people, at a cost of £600. All the girls seem to be wearing their Sunday best, I wonder how long their aprons stayed lovely and white.

Visible in the background is the first Wesleyan Methodist chapel, which was built in 1849 at the bottom of Drakehouse Lane. The site was donated by Mrs Green and building funds were raised by public subscription. The opening ceremony was performed by the Revd Samuel Dowsland Waddy DD, Governor of Wesley College, Sheffield.

Wesleyan Chapel & School, Beighton.   P.D.21

The second Wesleyan chapel was built in 1881 on land belonging to Lord Manvers, at a rent of £10 per year. The cost of the new chapel was £1,060 and it seated 225 people. It had to be rebuilt in 1905 at a cost of £2,380.

Beighton Primitive Methodist church on Robin Lane was built in 1890. It was designed to seat 200 people and cost £900 to build. This is the only Methodist church left in Beighton today.

The Gospel Hall on Eckington Road.

The first Catholic church was built in 1924 at a place known as Bate's Squire, just off the bottom of Drakehouse Lane. It was called St Gabriel's Hall and was opened by the Bishop of Nottingham. The wooden structure of the church was moved in 1946 to Manvers Road (where it is pictured) and was renamed the Church of Christ the King in 1950.

Six
Schools and Bedgreave

The Beighton Board School was built in 1880. It doesn't look much different today and is still full of children.

The earliest school at Beighton was opened in the 1700s, on West Street. In later years it was used as a reading room, then a cobblers shop and later was known as Starbuck Farm.

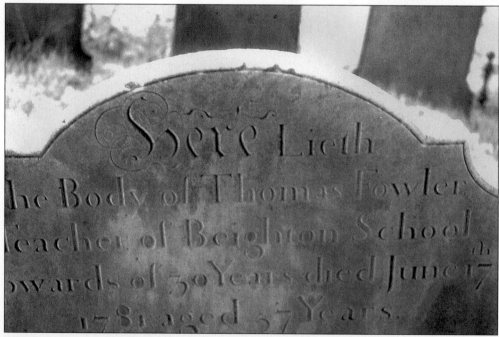

This gravestone stands in Beighton churchyard. It reads: 'Here lieth the body of Thomas Fowler teacher of Beighton School upwards of 30 years, died 17 June 1781. Aged 57 years.'

The second school to be opened was in Drakehouse Lane. It was built in 1854 at a cost of £800 and opened in 1855 with 150 children. Daniel Smith and his wife taught at the school. The author's grandfather had to pay to go there.

Tye Lane was the site of another school before state schools were introduced.

The Elms at the bottom of Queens Road was another private school known as Keelings School. It was converted into two houses in which the Harrisons and Smiths lived.

School Road in the early 1900s. There were not many houses there then.

Teachers in the senior school in 1947. Back row, from left to right: Miss Howson (school clerk), Mr E. Marsh, Mr H. McKie, Annie Naylor (née Hawkes), Mr R. Darker, Mrs N. Finney. Front row: Mr A. Large, Mr Harry May, Mr G. Hardy, Mr Cliff Wright, Mr C. Kirk.

How many children in the 1929-30 school year do you recognise here? The teacher is the very familiar Miss Ward of course. Back row, from left to right: -?-, -?-, Patrick Ducy, Arthur Hedley, Helen Staniforth, Geof Norburn, ? Crofts, -?-. Middle row: ? Holden, Frank Marshall, Dorothy Beardall, -?-, -?-, ? Riley. Front row: Ernest Taylor, George Lister, ? Whitehead, -?-, ? Marson, ? Tomlinson, Eddie Sparks, Miss Mary Ward.

We go up School Road and down Cow Lane and make our way down Meadowgate Lane to Bedgreave Mill, which was an ancient grist mill on the River Rother for grinding corn. It stood between Beighton and Killamarsh. It would have complimented the Beighton grist mill further down stream.

A further view of Bedgreave Mill and farm, now in Rother Valley Park. With the help of Beighton History Society we were able to prevent the demolition of the old buildings. We also found out that the place was much older than we had hitherto realised.

The Dawson sisters are sitting on the bank of the River Rother. The millers pause in their work for a moment in this pre-1900 view of Bedgreave Mill.

James Henry Dawson and his wife also lived at Bedgreave Mill. This, their gravestone is in the churchyard. He died at age 32 years, Mary Elizabeth at 51 years.

A different view of Bedgreave farm, now in the Rother Valley Country Park.

Some members of the Beighton Historical Society are seen here paying a visit to Bedgreave Mill in 1975 before its restoration.

Seven

Industry

A view of the railway station looking in the direction of Killamarsh. People often caught the train to Sheffield as it was much quicker than using the bus. During the summer season excursion trains to Cleethorpes were laid on, making popular cheap day outings for families.

Beighton station looking down the line to Woodhouse, c. 1900. The stationmaster, attired in peaked cap and overcoat, poses with his staff.

A new bypass and roundabout occupies the area where this humpback bridge stood. It formed part of the road leading out of Beighton over the River Rother to Swallownest.

The burnt out shell of Glovers flour mill stood on Mill Road which is now called Rotherham Road. The mill was destroyed by fire in 1897. In the foreground is the River Rother.

Among the men are Messrs White, Costello, Grant, Jones and Ward. These men worked at the flour mill in the 1890s.

The first coke ovens were built on the left hand side of Rotherham Road (going out of the village), at the side of the first Beighton Pit, which ceased to wind coal in 1886. Brookhouse Pit and the second lot of coke ovens were on the other side of the road. The coke oven chimney was 250ft high and was a well known landmark.

Frank Billam is pictured on the right, in front of one of the boilers at the coke ovens, c. 1912.

The second coke ovens. The 250ft chimney was demolished in 1982.

A night view of the coke ovens at Christmas time in 1975 shows the floodlights and other overhead lighting.

George Powell is seen here driving a loco for the coke ovens.

The sidings for Brookhouse coke ovens are now part of Rother Valley Park. The site of Beighton Castle, mentioned in a thirteenth-century charter, was close to this spot.

The construction of the second Beighton Colliery shaft was begun in 1902. Stan Fox's grandfather is the man holding the bucket.

Men working at Beighton Pit in the early 1900s; what about the head gear? The man leaning on his umbrella is obviously the managing director.

The output of Brookhouse Pits was 200,000 tons. The shaft was sunk in 1929 and in 1931 the pit bottom was formed in the Thorncliffe seam at a depth of 420 yards.

The sinking of Brookhouse Pit in 1929.

Mr Feek is one of the men seen coming off shift at Brookhouse Pit.

The men from the pit and coke ovens had to find alternative ways of getting home during the floods. This is Crown Terrace, the occupants had to live upstairs away from the water, sometimes for weeks at a time.

Water, water everywhere but not a drop to drink. The gasworks on the left found it hard to carry on working.

A train in the station in the 1930s. The flood water is level with the platforms.

94

There is a road somewhere! Men had to travel by boat to the colliery, but the closed gates of the level crossing indicate that the trains were still running.

Old Beighton Colliery with the old coke ovens in the background, in the 1920s. Workmen are pictured walking home through the floods.

Crown Terrace, a row of houses situated next to the Railway Inn.

Marshals traction engine is pictured helping out, *c.* 1925.

The gasworks on Rotherham Road can be seen just beyond the level crossing surrounded by flood water.

The cottages in the background formed the first Railway Inn prior to 1915, when Mr and Mrs Boaler and Wm Wells lived there. In later years 'Steamboat Bill' was a well known occupant.

Bill Ryder lived near the Railway Inn, he was affectionately known as 'Steamboat Bill'.

In 1958 the floods were so bad that water came right up the High Street. The last East Midland bus was stranded near the George & Dragon car park.

A further view of the floods in 1958.

Brookhouse Colliery
Pit Head Baths

THE
OPENING CEREMONY

will be performed on

SATURDAY, NOV. 24th 1951 at 3 p.m.

by

W. E. JONES, Esq., O.B.E., J.P.,

Vice-President of the National Union of Mineworkers
General Secretary, Yorkshire Area, National Union of Mineworkers

———

After the Opening Ceremony, the Pit Head Baths
will be open for inspection.

On Sunday, November 25th, between the hours of 2 p.m.
and 5 p.m. the Baths will be open for any employee who
wishes to bring his friends or relations to see them.

———

These Baths will be used for the first time by the
Night Shift on November 25th, 1951

The Brookhouse Pit Baths opened in 1951.

Eight
Transport and Wartime

We had three coaching companies in Beighton. Grant & McAllin's on Manvers Road, Sharpe Bros on West Street and Beck's on Queen's Road. This is Grant & McAllin's 'The Regent' which is about to take a party out for the day in 1924. Note the roll back cover which could be pulled forward to provide shelter in unsettled weather.

Mr and Mrs McAllin are photographed with a party of OAP's before the coach leaves for the day on an excursion.

Bernard McAllin with one of their coach's, The Empress, on Manvers Road.

An open topped coach belonging to Sharpe Bros of West Street is pictured, *c.* 1924.

Fred Sharpe was taking some friends to Hollinsend. Note the horn and the folded cover at the back.

Mr Beck's charabanc in the 1920s, he was taking Eddie Smith and family out to a party.

The first bus leaves from the bottom of Queen's Road in 1921. The bus took passengers as far as Intake, the fare being 4 d. The passengers then had to alight and continue their journey by tram from the Intake tram terminus into Sheffield.

This was the second bomb of the Second World War to be dropped on Britain and it came down in Woodhouse Lane. Fortunately it just missed the gas main.

The war comes to Beighton. This bomb was dropped in Meadowgate Lane in the 1940s but it didn't explode. It was later unearthed in 1977 by an excavator driver when the area became the site of an open cast mine. The Herman bomb weighed almost a ton and it was thought that its target was perhaps the nearby coke ovens.

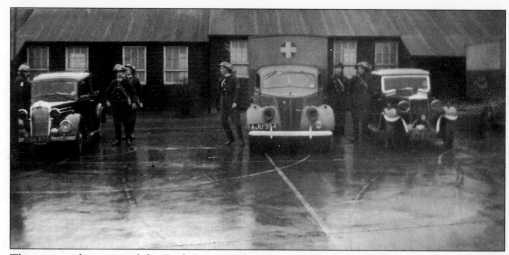

The men and women of the Red Cross are being put through their paces outside the school huts. The huts were used as the school during the day. We had an army camp on Eckington Road with ack-ack guns and search lights to give warning when enemy planes were in the vicinity.

The same place as pictured above, seen here with a full line of vehicles.

The ladies from the St Johns Nursing Division were all well turned out for an inspection parade.

Every week the Red Cross and the ARP wardens would train so that they would always be ready if needed.

Beighton Pit Home Guard is shown here being disbanded at Moorgate in Rotherham.

These are some of the ARP wardens testing their equipment.

Nine
People

We had a fair every year, during the second week of August. All the lads helped to erect the equipment just to get a free ride.

Harniess Bros fair came to Beighton in the 1920s. This was their Scenic Motor ride, with an ornate top and fairground organ, over which are the words promising, 'Our true intent is all for your delight'.

Beighton Gala, in 1953. The crowd is pictured on West Street, Mr Hardy can be seen in the background and Mr McKie stands in the middle of the children.

110

One of the floats in the 1953 gala. Julia Renshaw (co-author of this book) is the queen, pictured with Jean Ball, Barbara Durham, Mary Thorpe, Alan Brocklehurst, Eric Finney and John Oram.

Frank Turner is seen here in the grounds of Brookhouse School with his organ – the Organola.

Captain Johnson is on horse back at the end of School Road, following Money's van, in 1913. The van is advertising the Central Cinema.

Cookery day at Beighton School, in the 1930s. Back row, from left to right: M. Humble, Betty Crooks, Eileen Thorogood, M. Mallender, Sybil Walters, Zena Rowe. Front row: Eunice Freeman, Olive Hudson, Joan Grice, Joyce Whitham, Edna Antcliffe, Mary Sayles, Dorothy Siddall.

Red Cross workers during the war Mrs Lipp, Mrs McAllin, Mrs Havercroft, Mrs Bennett and Mrs Peat are pictured receiving a donation.

The Red Cross ladies are about to embark on a day trip. McAllin's 'Manvers Princess' coach was to be their transport.

MUM   NELLIE   IVY

ivy

Mrs Widdowson, Mrs Head and Mrs Neville were among some of the WI ladies helping with some fund raising. Back row, from left to right: Mrs Head, Mrs Chandler, Mrs Caterer, Mrs Widdowson, Mrs Tolley, Mrs Purdy, Mrs Holt, Mrs Gale. Front row: Mrs Fanthorpe, Mrs Neville, Mrs Rowbotham, Miss Rowbotham.

School plays at Christmas time in the 1930s. U. Walker, M. Sargent and D. Totty are among the players pictured here.

Among the actors seen here are: A. Spurr, D. Bland, B. Dawson and E. Stannard.

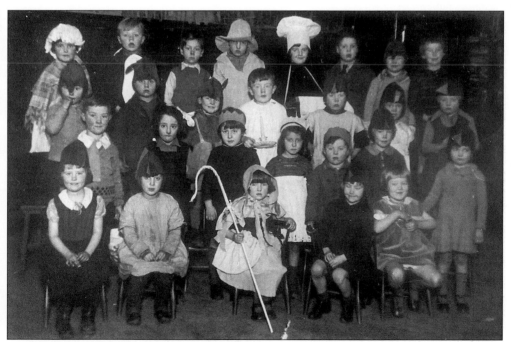

A school play of *Little Bo-Peep* in the late 1930s.

Galas and parades were held in 1925. This was the scene in front of Beighton School. Mrs Kane, Mrs Powell and Mrs Scott are some of the ladies who have joined in.

Beighton Gala was held in the recreation grounds. In the background the old George & Dragon can be seen.

Take your partners. M. Neilam, B. Stallard, V. Fanthorpe and D. Wood are some of the children pictured.

Beighton School concert in 1908. Among those present are: Elsie Pearson, Gladys Baker, Bade Turton, Reg Fewkes and Herbert Renshaw.

This looks like a ladies' day out. I hope it stayed fine as there was no cover on the charabanc. Mrs Noden, Miss Mirfin, Mrs Tomlinson and Mrs Rowbottom are some of the ladies pictured.

Many Beighton residents didn't want to be part of Sheffield. A train full of people travelled to London to object and to lobby MP's on the day the bill was read in parliament. Their efforts were to no avail as Beighton became a part of Sheffield in 1967. Reg Fewkes led the objectors as chairman of the parish council.

Mr Baden Turton, a well known and well liked figure in Beighton, was one of the parish councillors. He was also a Derbyshire county councillor.

Mr Money is seen delivering post in School Road, c. 1950.

Mr Money with his delivery van, a step up from the bicycle.

Beighton Cricket Club, 1938. Back row, from left to right: P. Saville, R. Barker, L. Swindell, R. Bright, S. Gibbs, N. Herberts, G. Cope, B. Whittaker, J. Harrison, F. Hook, J. Ambler. Front row: J. Rhodes, P. Roscoe, C. Whittaker, F. Taylor, B. Widdowson.

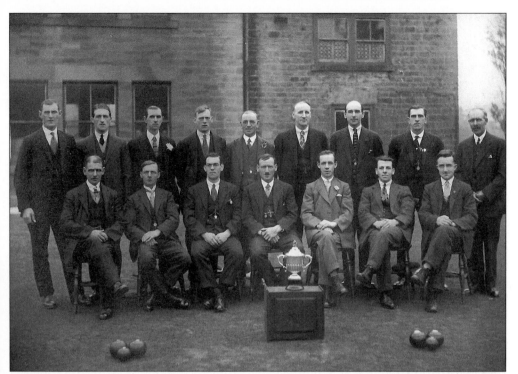

Beighton Miners Welfare Bowling Club, 1928. Back row, from left to right: F. Ballance (club secretary), J. W. Dent, G. Urwin, W. Stevenson, F. Vernon, W. Metcard, J. Bishop, L. Rackurn, G. Fox. Front row: J. Vernon (club president), H. Storer, T. Blackburn, W. Parkes (captain), L. Finney, J. Havenhand, A. Bartholomew.

Beighton Junior Football Club. H. Holden, F. Turner and A. Storey are a few of the club members seen here.

Beighton fire service, during the Second World War. Included among those pictured are: J. Bramall, K. Lancashire and V. Hancock.

The Snooker Club at Sothall Working Mens Club. There is still a snooker hall at Sothall today.

Miners Welfare Male Voice Choir sang on Cleethorpes pier, in the 1930s. The pier caught fire not long afterwards.

Queens Road Club games league in the 1950s. Mr Davis and Mr A. Brocklehurst are pictured with other team members.

Beighton School football team in 1916. Mr Felstead was the headmaster at that time and Mr J. Blackburn trained the team.

The Church Boys Brigade, 1917. Revd Maughan is in the centre. This is one of many groups that were photographed in front of the Major Oak tree at Edwinstowe.

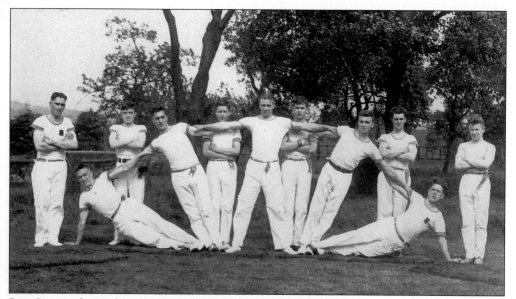

Ron Stannard puts the men through their paces at the Gym Club.

Beighton Miners Welfare Veterans Team 1935

I wonder if the present day Miners Welfare bowls team have amassed as many cups as the team of 1935.

Beighton Paper Mill workmen in 1924. Among them are Mr Gee, Frank Holden and G. Grant. Mr Haigh was the manager at the time.

The people of Allen Road enjoy a street party.

The WI ladies are pictured at Trenton Gardens; Mr Green drove the coach.

MUM   MRS S PURR

A Lady Day parade of the Catholic church on Robin Lane in the 1950s. The parish priest was F. Cardwell; Enid and Eileen Atack and Mary Turton are carrying the statue.

A concert at the Free Church on West Street, before it was pulled down. Elsie Stannard, Harry Rowbottom and Rosie Renshaw are three of the people in the group.

This concert was held c. 1915. We could not discover the names of any of the people pictured – perhaps you recognise some of them?